MARKETING CREATIVE
Hacks

- Ways for Subconscious Marketing -

by Mark
Zusmanovich

Marketing Creative Hacks

Ways for Subconscious Marketing

ISBN-13: 978-171729-896-6
ISBN-10: 1-717-29896-6

Edited and designed by Mark Zusmanovich

www.pentocreative.com

Give feedback on the book at:
mark@pentocreative.com

Twitter: @Mark_Zusman
Facebook: www.facebook.com/PentoCreative

First Edition

Printed in the U.S.A

*Dedicated to my beloved wife, **Dikla**, who is blindly supporting me, turning every wish of mine into a reality.*

*To my dear father, **Valery**, who has always guided me the right way, to find the area of my passion.*

- *Introduction* -

S tudies show that 90% of information transmitted to the brain is visual.[1] Articles with visual content get 94% more views and exposure.[2]

In this book, I'll show you how I've learned (still learning) the process to deliver fast, marketing creative designs that actually worked. I've come to an understanding that design is not just supposed to be "pretty" or appealing to the eye, or however you wanna call it.

In order to create a great design, I need first to create a great creative concept. And if I want to create a great creative concept, I need to learn the ways people think and feel, just like peeling layers of an onion. It's a combination of many different kinds of layers, working together to find the best solutions for specific needs and presenting it in the best way possible.

I hope this book will give you some ideas and practical tools for a drawing creative that will enter the subconscious and hypnotise your target audience into action.

Contents

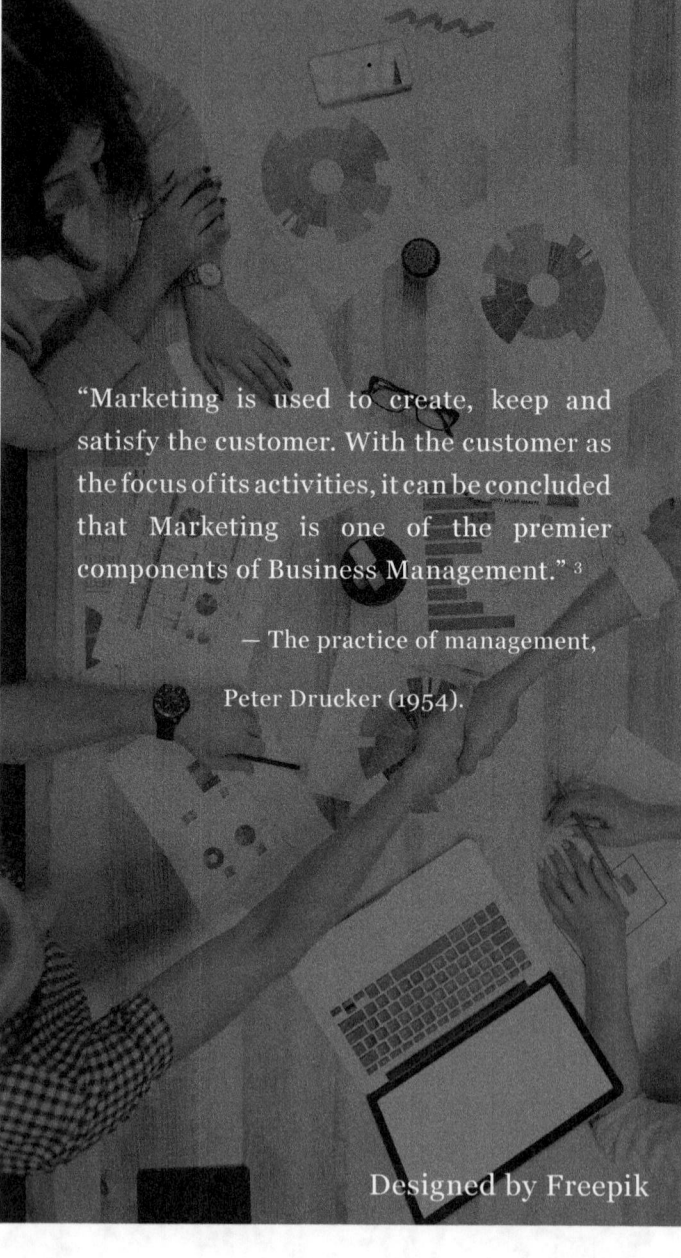

"Marketing is used to create, keep and satisfy the customer. With the customer as the focus of its activities, it can be concluded that Marketing is one of the premier components of Business Management." [3]

— The practice of management,

Peter Drucker (1954).

- One -

Marketing not Spamming

Most of my life I used to be disgusted by these polished, fast-talking salespeople. You're probably familiar with this feeling that you get when you enter a store and the salespeople are jumping on you, like sharks, trying to convince you that some product is on sale and you must buy it right now before it's too late.

One day it hit me. I didn't dislike the advertising industry or the amateur salespeople I ran into. It was simply because the offer wasn't presented to me at the right time, in the right place, with the right product I really needed. In other words, I wasn't the target audience and it felt like I was being spammed.

It's that spam, creating a bad name for advertising, salespeople and the whole marketing industry. If marketing can be described with the 4 P's (product, price, place and promotion), spam, for me, is delivering the wrong product, with the wrong price, to the wrong person in the wrong time (the 4 W's).

To have a better understanding of the marketing industry before we even get to design, we need to have a sneak peek at the past and learn how it all begun. We might mistakenly think that the principles of marketing, design and selling were invented somewhere in the 50's during the "Mad Men" times where advertising agencies had an extraordinary growth. As a matter of fact, since the early days of the caveman, drawings in caves and the days of the beginning of communication between human beings, marketing has been part of our evolution. If a caveman wanted to hunt a Mamut, he had to figure out how should he convince his neighbour to take this adventure.

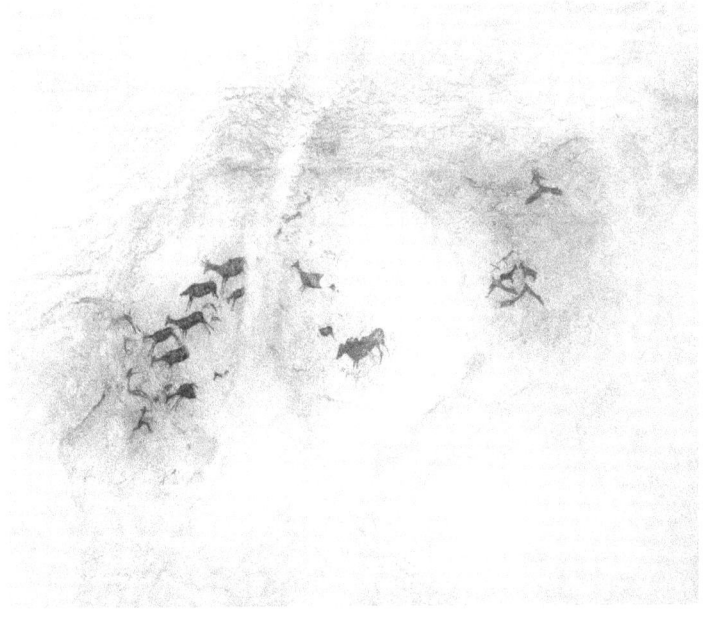

Johannes Gutenberg invented the printing press in 1450 and created a revolution of mass communication, and with it, mass advertising on newspaper. As time went by, the telegraph was invented by Samuel Morse in 1838 and in 1864, was the first ever recorded spam message.[4]

Just like the war between antivirus companies and the virus creators, with new technology we got new spam, new advertising channels and new marketing strategies.

I'm not saying all advertising is spam, quite the opposite, some advertising is really a lifesaver when it's presented in the right place. If you're driving for three hours, for example, you're tired and dehydrated and you see a sign saying "Thirsty? Turn right for coffee". It is the right place and the right product which makes the promotion of this very easy. When you figure out all parts of the equation, you don't have to sell and persuade, being spammy.

Travel image created by Freepik

When Marketing is done correctly, the target audience will reach the product without any further persuasion.

Since I was a little child, I saw that there's a pattern. A magical triangle. Companies paid money for ads on channels that created "free" content on media like television, radio or press, but something wasn't working so well with that system. Not everyone was interested in all products the commercials presented.

Back in the early 90's, there was only one TV channel with all the commercials in the world, news, cartoons and soap operas.

I remember, as a little boy, it was so confusing to see it. I had no interest in washing powder or a vacuum cleaner so most of the commercials weren't relevant for me. In time, more channels appeared. This way, toy companies could advertise on the children's channel while the washing powder companies could advertise on adults channels and hit their target audience in the right place and in the right time.

Companies became more and more sophisticated. They came to an understanding that they could produce their own content and this way, attract their target audience without even advertising much.

In 1895, The John Deere company created *"The Furrow"* Magazine that had content about farming. The director at that time realised that the farmers need a reliable source of information, so the farmers would read the magazine and buy John Deere products. John Deere didn't even try to promote itself in this magazine and the words "John Deere" appeared in the magazine just a few times, and I'm talking about going back during a 120 years period. [5]

In 1950 a soap opera named "The Guiding Light" was invented by, no other than "Procter & Gamble" corporation, simply because they understood the target audience, the place and the time they could be found and figured that the best way to approach them would be through soap operas. [5]

So it looks like this "big secret" was out a long time ago, but somehow, it's ignored. Maybe out of convenience, a lot of big companies still don't create content, and their only marketing strategy is "brand awareness" with television commercials, radio and newspaper ads.

The minute the internet emerged, the picture has completely changed. There is more and more information produced every second and more channels we can get this information from.

Once we had a small number of channels for advertising and every company wanted to be on the same channel at the same hour. Today we are overflowed with technological platforms for consuming information, whether it's written like blogs, audible like podcasts, vlogs for video blogs, and social networks like Facebook and Twitter for mass communication. Gary Vaynerchuk once said: "Instagram and Snapchat, and Twitter and Facebook are the new CBS, NBC, and Showtime." [6]

Times have changed but we as humans still operate the same. The same old techniques that were invented, or should I say discovered, regarding the human mind and the way it operates, are relevant today as well.

We still need to find the right product for the right people in the right place to promote to. It's just that the place has changed and now it's online. The promotion techniques have changed, and the people have much more options and information resources to go to and to compare. If once we could just say, "Hi, this is my product and you should buy it" and it could be probably enough because there was no other channel, so no one never knew there was any alternative product at all.

Nowadays, we have to try harder. We are now having now the biggest ADHD crisis humanity have ever faced.

Everything is super easy to buy and can be found online in seconds. If we want to get our audience's attention, we must be creative. We need to connect with them.

If we want to make our target audience like us for who we are and what we represent, we need to draw them in by speaking in their language and triggering their emotions instead of just telling them about our product, because there are billions of people telling them about their products, trying to convince them every day to buy something they don't really need. And now we're back to spamming again.

- *Two* -

What is Design?

When I was in junior high I had to choose which subjects I want to learn for my matriculation exam. One of the professionals was Graphic Design. My parents suggested I take it since I like art and I like to draw. It didn't take too long to understand that these are two completely different endeavours.

I always get these questions, especially from anyone who is not familiar with this industry (like kids and elder relatives), when they hear I'm a designer:

"What does a designer do, exactly?"

"Are you a painter?"

"Is it like an artist?"

Actually, there's a big difference between art and design and between an artist and a designer. Some even say that they are the exact opposite of one another.

The Basics

If we search on Wikipedia for a "Design" we get: "Design is a part of the communication arts, a design is something you plan to create, it communicates to the viewer or user a visual and emotional message to change or guide through an emotional connection with a product or service enhancing their experience of the product or brand." [7]

In other words, "Design" is a way of guiding people to take action or enhancing the connection with a brand.

If were search for "Art" on the other hand we get: "Art is a diverse range of human activities in creating visual, auditory or performing artefacts (artworks), expressing the author's imaginative or technical skill, intended to be appreciated for their beauty or emotional power." [8]

See, while a designer has his target audience and specific goals in mind, the only thing that matters to the artist is to be appreciated for what he wants to communicate. The only thing Art and Design have in common is that they both try to get to somebody's feeling or create some emotion.

We should never refer to design as beautiful, pretty or ugly. Instead, we should ask ourselves if this is a design that will work. Does this design provoke an action, such as pushing a button, buying the product, or donating to a nonprofit organization?

Beauty is a subjective emotion. Some might see a piece of art and claim it to be the most beautiful thing they saw in their entire life, while others might say they didn't like it at all.

We can interpret Art in many ways. Every observer will get a different emotion looking at art, either good or bad. We can try to figure out what has the artist felt at that very moment of creation, but we can never know what the designer felt designing the Ad.

We can only know what we feel about that design and did we take action because of that. We might even like it less or not like it at all, but if the ad or the site made us want to press a button or fill the form, it means that the designer has done a good job.

Even if the Ad made you feel upset or angry, this might be the whole purpose of that ad. If a "Greenpeace" Ad makes us want to become activists or share vegan promotional materials, that could be very controversial, but if the audience took action because of that, the campaign was successful.

The Artist usually creates the emotions without any target or agenda to make the observer actually do something or buy something (except his own art in some cases), while the designer's number one goal is exactly that. A good design makes us feel something and then go and take action, even if the goal is to make a better connection to a brand (brand awareness). Eventually, the main goal is to motivate to action.

Advertising companies spend millions on researching the human mind, trying to understand and influence human emotions, routines and habits, and to have a better picture about what style of an Ad should be created and what time frame and placement the Ad should be presented to make it most effective.

— By Billy Hathorn - Own work, CC BY-SA 3.0.

The Right Questions

We, as creatives and designers, should ask the right questions about whatever we are asked to design.

If it's an Ad, we should ask:

"Where is it gonna show up?"

Because there should be a difference between a big billboard Ad in the city and a bus stop advertisement.

The city Ad is going to get just a few seconds of exposure to the driver, along with all other things, disturbing him from the road. Which means, it should really stand out and must be very clear with its message. Maybe just a few words and a very clear and sharp image, or no image at all. We must not make the drivers try to interpret what they see, by staring at it for too long, while driving.

A bus stop Ad, on the other hand, might get an hour of being stared at, which means we can add some reasonable amount of text to it and play with the visual's details as we wish, even if it's a much smaller proportion Ad, than the highway billboard.

Designed by Freepik

Therefore, a Facebook Ad should be different from a sponsored Ad on a news website, an e-commerce website, on Instagram or Snapchat.

People go to Facebook to socialize with their friends, see cute animals and "food porn".

Nobody goes on Facebook to see promotional Ads.

If we need to design a Facebook Ad, we must keep that in mind and try to make it look "organic" as possible, instead of a hard sell promotional ad. If we have to design an Ad that will show up on a news website, it should look just like one of the news articles on the website, instead of just a colour changing, tall banner on the side of the screen, because people just don't see them anymore.

An artist doesn't ask these questions. A painter doesn't keep in mind the observer's state in the moment of exposure to his art, nor does he really analyze the difference of one gallery's benefits to another, before he starts crafting his art, just like most companies do, before they approach a designer.

Good design can be actually measured by numbers. If we change the background of a landing page from white to black, for example, and from that very moment, we would find out the page converts 20% more, that means that black background "works better" than the white background, in that specific landing page. It doesn't matter if we like black or white, the fact is "it converts better".

Good art is an art that leaves a mark. An art that we remember and appreciate, but since there is no conversion act in art, we can't really measure, what art is better or what art works best.

Art and Design are both trying to get to our emotions, but art usually doesn't try to get us taking action like design does. Even if the goal is to enhance the connection to a brand, we still have to take some kind of action to do that, whether, by following it on social networks or buying and using it's products, because of some commercial we saw on television. Unless it's designed this way, for the observer to not take any action, which is also an action...

The artist, unlike the designer, creates his art to express his emotions, or create them for others, regardless the audience's origins, while a designer has to learn and completely understand his target audiences' world, with every new project, if he wants his campaign to be successful as possible.

- Three -

Design Process

A s a self-employed marketing designer, I had the privilege to work with a very big variety of different types of clients, whether it was a one-person business such as private lawyers, real estate agents or a construction engineers, small companies with 10 to 50 employees and all the way to major companies of more than 100 employers, like education institutes and pharmaceutical companies.

They all had all kinds of different projects. Some needed a new website, some needed a logo and a whole branding style development and some asked for some social activity. I've noticed that the questions I had to ask them where pretty much the same and my job becomes much easier, the more I follow this process of asking the right questions, guiding the client to the right strategy, needs to be executed for the best outcome.

Homework

I know it sounds funny but before I even get to a meeting with a client, the first thing I do is homework, and when I say homework, I mean research. I go online and search for every source of information regarding this new client.

"What do they do?"

"Do they have competition?" (hopefully)

"What is their competitors' strategy?"

"What is their social activity?"

The first talk with a client, whether he approached me or I approached him, is an "interview". I get to know him and he gets to know me. Who he is and what has he done in his life?

I know it sounds like a waste of time for a lot of people who like to get straight point, but I have learned that this little "chitchat" makes you really understand a person, get to know him, his taste and find out what he would or would not like to do for his business.

Step two is an interview for its business:

"What is your business?"

"Who are your best clients?"

"What is the problem your business can solve?"

Even if we think we know the answers, after our little research, it's highly important to ask them because, whatever we think we learned and already know, the business owner probably knows better, since he dedicated his life to it and shows you their perspective so you know what he thinks of himself and his business.

Whether a client wants a Facebook page, website or even a YouTube channel, when I meet my new client in the first time, the first question I ask him is:

"What is the main goal of the project?"

Obviously, there's a big difference between a website that is trying to get clients on the phone and a website showing the address or a map for local business.

Usually, the bigger the business, there is a pretty precise strategy for whatever you need to design for them. In this case, you'll probably be guided throughout your design and creative, according to the companies strategies and goals, but even then, we must politely suggest our point of view, even if it appears to be the opposite to whatever they are suggesting, as professionals in our field of expertise and according to our experience and researches for better results.

The same way, they know a lot better in their field of expertise, we as creatives, have been exposed to the best marketing strategies, during our career, so we could suggest an idea we saw of some award-winning campaign.

The smaller the business, (one person show in particular), the questions needed to be asked are going to be much deeper. This is where it's getting really interesting. You see, small business owners don't have a marketing plan, a social media specialist or advertising strategist.

A business owner might have heard from a friend that he needs Snapchat because this is the next big thing, but this friend has forgotten to mention that the average age of Snapchat users is between 18 to 24, so if this client is a chiropractor and he's targeting middle-aged men with back problems, Snapchat might not be the best solution for him.

This is why we should always try to guide our client with the right questions to the right answers to get the best outcome for him.

Social Burger

Once, I was asked to design a facebook page for a fast food restaurant. He said that he "heard" that he needs a Facebook fan page, so he approached me.

I said: "That's great! do you have a long-term strategy for Facebook?"

He said: "No, I just want a *plain* Facebook page".

I tried to explain that a Facebook page is not a poster nor a website. A *plain* Facebook *fan* page will not get any traffic nor fans. Facebook is a social living platform where we can follow and stay connected to our friends and family. It's all about sharing entertainment. We have to engage people to take action if we want our posts or pages to be shown, found and get bigger exposure as possible.

We were thinking about ways to make the followers share and comment on our posts so they get more views.

At first, he proposed to make a competition in which the participants are going to share a story about the best burger they had in that restaurant.

The winner will get the free burger. The problem was that after this competition, only one client is going to show up to get a free burger. Maybe he'll get a drink or his friends will buy something, but eventually, we were thinking about taking the competition concept and just sharpen it the little bit to make it much more profitable.

I proposed to create a competition in which, the participants would have to go to the restaurant, take a picture of them having their favourite burger.

Then, they are going to have to post on the restaurant's Facebook page and ask the friends to like and share it. The person with the most amount of likes and shares is going to get a meal for two.

This way the participants are going to input content in our page for us, then they're going to share it with their friends and family + they are all going to have to visit the restaurant and get a burger, just for participating in this little social game.

Personal Taste

It is very easy for us sometimes to fall into that "service provider" state of mind, doing everything the clients asks us to do without asking any questions.

One day it hit me, "If a business owner doesn't like red, it doesn't mean he can't use red in any of his products or promotional materials, not even when its completely necessary." Obviously, I can't force a client to use red, but it's my responsibility to let him know that every colour has a variety of emotional effects so it will be very difficult to make our users feel danger, passion or heat without the red colour.

If the client is a lawyer and he likes motorcycles and guns and needs a website for his law firm, he can't just ask us to add a few motorcycles and guns on his law firm website (This is actually a true story).

It took me decades trying to explain the needs of

his target audience and how people who look for a lawyer are people in time of need, searching for help.

Motorcycles make us feel very energetic, dynamic and adventurous, unlike a law firm that has to have some calm, classic, respected and maybe even a bit serious feel to it as if we are entering a clinic for our problems. A motorcycle has a completely opposite effect.

Collaborating not Providing

Every designer has been through that routine. A client asks for a website or an ad. The designer provides two or three options for designs. The client picks one, in the best case scenario, sometimes he doesn't pick anything at all.

Why does that happen?

There's something about the way human beings are wired, that makes us evaluate less, things that we get free. If a client asks for a website and he gets 3 examples for a website layout, before he even signed a paper or paid anything, he is still in the "free" state of mind so he usually wouldn't care much for either one of them.

Whoever the client is, I make sure he is completely aware and being a part (as much as he can) of my process. I shared with him everything I've discovered in my research about him and his competitors. I ask him to send me examples of websites he likes or dislikes.

Even if it's a website about aliens and it has nothing to do with his occupation, I ask him to let me know, what he liked and disliked in it.

I send him the colour palettes I was thinking about, explaining every colour's purpose and why I picked it. Sign him up for a contract and ask for an advance payment to make him committed to this project as much as I am.

Make the client collaborate with you instead of just sending him 3 options.

This collaboration makes clients feel like they're part of this project and that we're building it together. It makes the clients much more attached to the project and most chances he'll like it more and feel more connected to the project, trying to help as much as he can, making it work, instead of searching for flaws.

Sometimes business owners think they need something but don't really understand why they need it or how it's supposed to work.

I'm sure you know about a business that created a website and nothing came of it.

It's because the website is not advertised properly and there's a chance that this particular business doesn't even need a website at all. Maybe a youtube channel or an Instagram account will do better.

Whatever the business is about, collaborate with him to find out what he really needs for his business, what content he could provide and what is the best strategy to put it on the market for best results.

- *Four* -
Creative Thinking

A lot of creatives ask this question about how to start from a blank document and dive to this creative process to get a well-designed product that you feel whole with, whatever this product might be. We are all human and we all had our times, in which we were staring at the monitor and nothing came up.

In time, I've discovered that there's this same, simple process for every product, we would like to design, whether it's a website, an app or a promotional campaign. There are a few steps every designer and creative should take before he begins to make his work much easier.

Topic Research

In my opinion, we as creative people should be familiar with the specific sector we are designing for, whether it's agriculture, medicine or law.

I'm not saying that every time I design a law firm website, I'm getting a law degree, but I have to make some basic research of this specific expertise, trying to understand this world I'm designing for, as much as I can, even if I've never been a lawyer or an attorney.

I have to be familiar with the specific language they use, their favourite colours and maybe even their hobbies, in order to have a better understanding of what will make them feel "home". This way it will be easier triggering their emotions.

When I had to design an architecture company website, I've searched for architecture on Wikipedia first, to have a general view of where and why did architecture emerge and what kind of different architectural styles are out there?

My next step was to Google architecture websites and I got an endless number of examples for all kinds of styles. This helped me to see the colour palettes, the compositions and the typography mostly used. This way I had a pretty clear guideline to get started.

I'm trying to do my best to become the target audience myself.

There's an old saying about the fact that if one wants to sell some product to another person, he should be using this product himself if he wants to successfully sell this product. I know for a fact that if I want to make a great converting campaign, I have to feel what my target audience feel and know what they know. This way (possibly the only way) I could know, what will drive them and get the most effective actions out of them.

It might sound obvious, but if I'm asked to create a "high-class" real estate ad about some big private houses, and I know nothing about high-class houses, it would be probably very hard for me to produce the right moving concept for my target audience, because there's a very good chance, I know nothing about this specific target audience.

It's not about getting that house whether I can or can not afford it. It's about getting to know the people who are interested in private houses and what moves them.

Consuming

My ways to become the target audience itself, are actually pretty simple. First I start with consuming the product or service, if possible.

If it's a spa massage boutique that needs to be rebranded, I go and take a massage session myself.

This way I really "feel" and get to know the business. I start to follow biggest massage clinics and try to understand their services. I try to find the difference and what makes my client so unique and special. I join Spa Facebook groups if I can, and sign up for Spa newsletters. Follow their email sequence and offers. This way, I get to know their competitor's strategy and style. I search for "Spa" on every social network I can, like Instagram, Pinterest, YouTube and Twitter to get inspired by different spa visuals and content types to help me produce my own content and concept for a good campaign that will stand out.

Avatar

Think about your best customer or your clients' perfect customer.

"What does he do?"

"Where does he hang out?"

"What is their gender?"

Maybe even: "What is their salary?"

Good avatar definitions can make our work much easier. I usually try to name avatars to make them feel realistic as possible and I really try to imagine this person, his needs and desires.

"What will make him buy a specific product?"

I search for friends and family or have anything to do with spa or massage and try to figure out where they hang out, what information they consume and what social networks do they prefer?

If you have all of these answered, or at least most of it, you can get a pretty clear picture of a person named "Hannah", who has three kids and a very demanding job. She loves her job and she loves her family, but from time to time she likes to take a break from the routine and take a minute for herself in this amazing Spa Boutique.

Her husband is a hard-working man who works 9-to-5 driving every day in the car for at least an hour, and we should know this because maybe would like to target the husband as our target audience and try to make him buy his wife a massage session as a gift. See, there are no rules and everything is possible. Creativity is the key, but this avatar definition can really help us get creative with our design products, whether it's websites, branding or just a social ad.

The
"Three Holy Grounds"

The most powerful ads have three layers. The first one is the background, which is responsible for the environment and the general feel. The second one is the foreground, which is basically, the main idea and the most important thing we want to be noticed.

The third one is the middle ground, that is usually forgotten, but this "middle ground" makes the whole thing look completely different.

The middle ground is the link connecting the background with the foreground and making it all work together. It could be a figure that's pointing on the text or the button, it could be some product like an iPhone with your app on it or a person using the product, whether it's an image or an illustration.

These "middle ground elements" are very boosting purchases percentage.

This is the reason why in software promotional materials, there will almost always be some kind of box showing this software, even though, it's a virtual product and there is no actual hardcover box with a "software" in it or a book picture representing an e-book without the actual book.

— Mockup psd created by Zlatko_plamenov - Freepik.com

Middle ground elements that work best in most times are female figures, female faces, babies and everything else cute in general and strong figure you could relate to or would like to follow, like a hero.

Eye contact with the viewer and a figure pointing or looking straight at the button do also a huge effect of calling to action. Middle ground can also be an element that you talk about in the text. If my ad is about Coffee, I'd show them the mug. If it's describing a huge gift box, I would probably show this gift box.

There are millions of different ways of designing and infinite numbers of ads' styles in Google and obviously, you can't just copy someone's else's ad but this little research I do gives me a pretty good picture of what is common, what traditions people have and what is the general look and feel of the specific occupational field. In some cases, it would be a great idea to join some facebook groups about the specific field, just to see what they talk about, how they talk and what drives them the most.

With that in mind, before I even open a design software, I research the field, take ideas, become the audience and always try to find my own interpretation that can allow me to stand out from all the other competitors.

Our challenge as creatives, designers and business owners is to combine the style of our specific brand, mix it with the style of a certain campaign or the story we want to tell and the emotions we want to trigger and put inside some extra mark of our own to make it stand out more than our competition.

- Five -

Composition Hacks

A Good composition creates a balanced and pleasing image that guides and leads the observer's eye to wherever it's supposed to go. As such, it is extremely important, especially in marketing creative and design, to guide the viewer to the right place and take the right action.

There are many rumours about the right composition and some magical formulas of some kind that calculates the specific place, in which every element will mesmerise people.

The fact is that there is no perfect single composition but there are many different guidelines for compositions. The problem is that the magical formula will work only if we have all the ingredients. Things like hierarchy, alignment, repetition and space. If we ignore one of them the whole composition will be unbalanced and generally will not feel solved.

I like to divide the composition into two lists of rules and guides. The list of rules will have three main rules that every design must have in order to get a good composition. The second is the "Nice to have" guides. They can help us with our decisions for compositions but we can create great compositions without following them.

Composition Guides

There are a few compositional structures that are usually used in marketing especially where we need to be very precise with our message since we have our goals and targets. It's not just about making things look good.

The Rule of Thirds

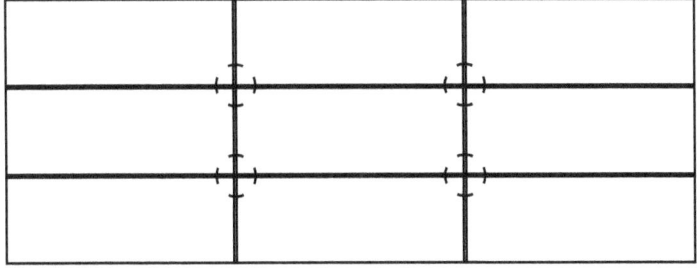

If we split our canvas into three horizontal and three vertical parts which are completely identical, we will get four "hotspots" where the lines cross each other, creating points of interest.

It's just the way human beings see things and decide what looks better and feels balanced. When we follow this rule, and place our main elements on these four intersections "hotspots", they will look pleasant to the eye and draw us in.

The role of thirds is used a lot in movies, art and architecture and it is great for marketing design since it's so easy to follow. We can place a figure ("The Middle Ground") on two of the hotspot on one side, while the text and the button on the other two hotspots of interest.

The golden ratio

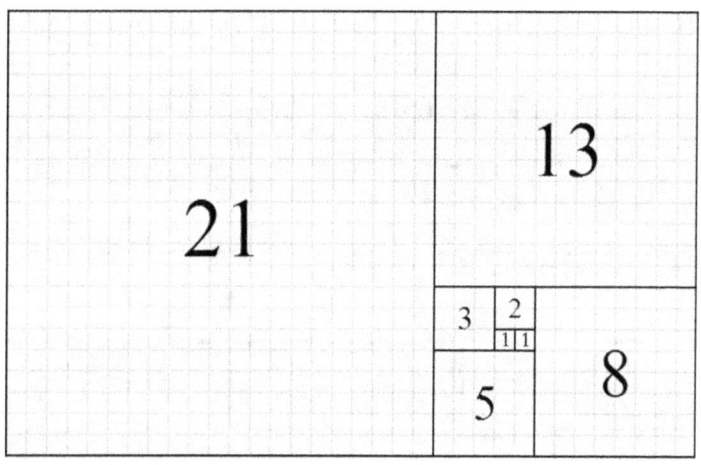

— Fibonacci sequence. [9]

Usually is mistaken with the role of thirds but it is a completely different composition.

The golden ratio is usually seen in the nature on animals like snails, plants and even can be found in space.

In mathematics, the Fibonacci numbers are the numbers in the following integer sequence, called the Fibonacci sequence, and characterized by the fact that every number after the first two is the sum of the two preceding ones: 1,1,2,3,5,8,13,21...[10]

— Leonardo da Vinci used the golden ratio in his paintings including the "Mona Lisa" ("La Gioconda").

The golden ratio is based exactly on these series of numbers. It might be a bit difficult trying to fit our design into this golden ratio golden line but the most mesmerising and breathtaking design composition is based exactly on that.

"Mathematicians since Euclid have studied the properties of the golden ratio, including its appearance in the dimensions of a regular pentagon and in a golden rectangle, which may be cut into a square and a smaller rectangle with the same aspect ratio."
   - Strogatz, Steven (September 24, 2012).
   "Me, Myself, and Math: Proportion Control", New York Times.

   - Golden ratio used on Twitter.com

- Golden ratio used on National Geographic website

In general, if we just place part of our design on one-third of the page and the other part of it on the other 2/3 of the page, most chances are, it will look aesthetic and balanced in some magical way.

There are a lot of different variations of composition styles and structures like "Pyramid" in which we place our main element, on the top middle of our image and everything else, following down and to the sides, creating a shape of a pyramid.

"Symmetric" in which we reflect everything we can to the second half of our image, creating a mirror effect. "Central composition" in which we can just place the elements in the center from top to bottom.

We can always create our own rules and structures as long as it looks balanced and focused especially when dealing with marketing design and creative.

In cases, there are a lot of elements that are needed to be shown and a lot of ideas to communicate, we would like to prioritise the elements and the ideas.

My way to deal with it is by placing all elements on my canvas making them small enough to fit. Then I try to find the most important elements and start enlarging it while making everything else smaller.

This way we can play with the sizes of the elements, creating a hierarchy, presenting the importance of the element, by its size. Sizes of elements can be a great guide for the attention of the observer.

If the ad is about sunglasses and a gift, I first try to decide which one is more important, the sunglasses or the gift. In this case, for example, we would present big sunglasses and a small gift box.

Some mistakenly make the gift as the main focal element, but the truth is, most people already know that there are no free gifts and usually when they see a huge gift box they tend to ignore it.

In music, when balancing a song, one of the ways to reach balance is to get the volume to a very, very low level, until you can barely hear it. When doing so, you can hear very clearly, whether the bass is too high or are there some loud overlapping sounds like flutes, adjusting them. This way we can balance the song pretty easily and make all instruments work together and not fighting for attention and disturbing each other.

Same way, one of my tricks to make sure everything is working together in my composition, for every kind of design, is to simply zoom out as much as possible until I barely see it, in a size of a stamp.

When you zoom out, you can see very clearly what stands out the most and what elements disappeared completely and are not noticeable enough.

Another great way to check composition is to flip the canvas horizontally and see if it still makes sense. When flipping the canvas, the text doesn't have meaning anymore and becomes lines and shapes.

This way we can really see the composition problems and fix them without being distracted by the text, the idea and the creative.

Composition Rules

Every design must take in count these 3 basic rules that if we miss one of them, our design simply won't be as effective.

First Rule:
Pick one focal element to stand out the most

Two focal elements are usually used if we want to give them equal significance like in a boxing ad, presenting two fighters, for example.

I'm not saying we need to have one element in our designs, I'm saying we need to pick one of them to stand out the most. Much like hierarchy, we must find out which element is more important so we know where to place it to preserve or empower its importance. So many designs fail just because they didn't follow this first rule and have too many focal elements or none of them at all.

Our focal element can be a lot of elements like a flock of sheep but they all have to compliment each other and not to fight for our attention as viewers.

We could even place them all in one place but take

just one sheep and put it outside of the flock to make it stand out, creating more interest and curiosity or blur all flock of sheep except one focused sheep, for example.

Second Rule:
The structure of the elements

Basically, it's the way to organise elements in a pleasing way. The "Composition Guides" can help us do it but "Composition Guides" are just one piece of the puzzle and you don't even need to follow them.

We can create our own structure of elements as long as it is aligned in the right way, there's a logical repetition and generally looks "pleasing".

The best way to check if our structure of elements is good is to simply ask ourselves and other people,

"Does it work for us?"

If it does, it will probably work. Either we accidentally followed the "Composition Guides" or might even create one of our own. The bottom line is that as long as it looks pleasing and balanced for most people, most chances are, our target audience will feel the same way.

Third rule:
Balance your design

This is probably the most common rule, not only in composition, but also in typography and colour.

Balance is one of the most important rules for making our design work.

In composition, we see balance as the weight of elements in our image. If there is a big element on one side of your image there must be at least a small element on the left side, so the image remains balanced. [11]

- Six -

Colour/Color Issues

We as human beings have the primitive ability to interpret colour meanings by the emotions we get when we see it.

In nature, most poisonous fruits are either red or yellow like Berries and European Spindle. Poisonous animals are usually marked with red and yellow colours like Death Stalker Scorpion, Brazilian Wandering Spider etc.

— Yellow Deathstalker in Negev Desert, Israel. [12]

So colour interpretation is very important for our survival as humans, right?

Cultural Differences

Throughout history, every culture created its own interpretation of colours based on beliefs, religions, local nature, weather and the general colours of the landscape like yellow deserts or snow white mountains. The seasons made us interpret colours by their "warmth" so blue usually symbolizes cold while red and orange symbolize warmth.

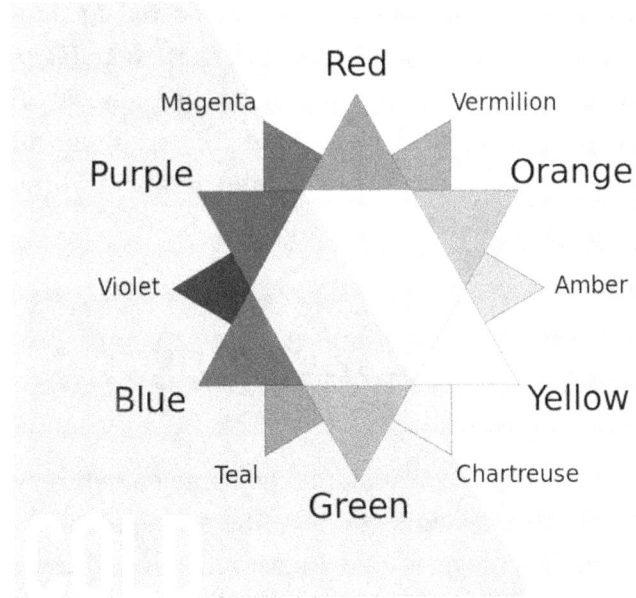

— Color star. [12]

The red colour in the western civilization is interpreted completely different from the interpretation it is given in the far east like China.

In China red is a colour of joy and good fortune so it's used until today for weddings and holiday celebrations. Red is strictly forbidden at funerals as it is the colour of happiness.

Different cultures don't even name the colours in the same way. In English, there are 11 words for colours while the Russian language has 12 (Light Blue = Galuboy).

In the Chinese culture black is the colour of heaven. This is why the black colour is interpreted to be a holy colour. Unlike the Westerners that wear black for funerals, and white for weddings, the Chinese, on the other hand, wear black and red for weddings and white for funerals since white is interpreted in China as the colour of mourning.

Double Meaning

Different cultures interpret the same colour very differently, but this is just one of the problems.

We tend to interpret colours very differently from one another, even if two people from the same country or even the same city, could respond completely different to the same exact colour.

While some see green as the colour of growth, nature and prosperity, maybe even positivity, others may see it as the colour of greed. As a matter of fact, Every colour has a mass variety of feelings and interpretations created by itself. The right use of the colour can get the right emotion triggered. A red dot has a different effect than a whole red background.

When we approach design, we must take into account so many variations to make it work. The culture it's presented to, the different interpretations that specific colour produces and the right amount of it, and the time and the placement it is going to appear in.

If our target audience is a Chinese man for example, and he's going to see our ad on Facebook at 21:00 pm, we might want to use certain colours to talk in his language and make him feel as much at home and comfortable as we can.

Placement is one of the most important factors for choosing the right colors. If it's really on Facebook, according to the previous example, there is a theory that says that colors work best on Facebook are red-orange and yellow so if we are targeting China, we must investigate and be sure that the colors are used properly according to what our target audience feels about it.

For example, an ad that is completely red might reflect danger or high-energy or passion for a Westerner, the same exact add is going to create feelings of joy and fortune in the far east.

Saturation

The way I try to treat these interpretation problems is by playing with brightness and saturation until I manage to create a decent balance.

Much like in composition, there must be a balance in our colour saturation. If we use highly saturated, vivid red for a background, in most cases the content will drown in this background color no matter what emotion we were trying to get, but if we use a little less saturated red and add a little bit of black for dark red, velvet or add white to make it pinkish, it will stand out less and the won't steal as much of focus, but still will be able to provide some of the emotions, simple red would provide.

Usually, we even have to make our target audience feel a combination of a few emotions at once, but if we use red and green together in the same exact amount, they will probably fight each other for attention and the result will not be as pleasing, but if we take one of them get it darker or a little brighter and use less space with them, for example, instead of getting half page red and half green, we would use a third of dark green and 2/3 of bright red, they will suddenly stop disturbing each other and start complementing the whole composition.

Actually one will make the other stand out while we will still have the emotions of both colours if we would like. If we have decided to use vivid saturated text, we must use either very dark or a very bright background colour.

When choosing a colour, we must take into account the feelings it provides for the specific target audience we are designing for. Otherwise, we could provide a completely different interpretation and a mistaken emotion that not only will not be successful but will also anger our target audience and associate a feeling we never meant to be associated with.

- Seven -
Master of Light

J ohannes Vermeer was given the name "Master of Light" as he was using his colours to produce lightened scenes, manipulating shadows and colours making his pieces of art so mesmerizing. [13]

He actually designed his paintings in such a precise way that it feels like every drop of colour has its own purpose, by a certain, specific place he placed them, creating emotions just like a well-calculated design with strategy and goals.

Manipulating Reality

Vermeer lived in the 15th century and was already using the colour theory essence and the composition rules.

He was actually manipulating the reality in order to improve his art, just like in the painting "The Art of Painting" in which, he didn't complete the right leg of the canvas holder of the painter in sake of balance or the "Girl with a Red Hat" in which he created a green background and a green shadow on the girls face to make the hat stand out. In real life, the girl's hat should probably be producing a red shadow on her face instead of a green one.

Sometimes it can be a great idea to manipulate the reality and in our design to make it more powerful and to present our idea better.

Sometimes only by the shadow, we can produce the exact emotion we wish for. In horror movies, a shadow is used as if the light comes from the bottom of the figure, which produces a very dramatic and tensed scene.

If we place a small object in the middle of the screen it will look as if the object is floating in space and we would not be able to determine its size or weight, but if we add the shadow of this subject in the bottom, it will look static and get that feeling of a physical object that has actual weight.

By manipulating the shadows in the right way we can get a very precise result. If I have a figure and I really want this figure to stand out and pop-up out of the screen, I usually add a shadow with a little bit of skew, which creates an illusion that this figure is moving towards us.

If it's a tiny small round shadow right underneath the object, the object will feel bigger or even heavier, while placing a shadow a little farther from the object, will make the object feel like it's jumping in the air.

If the shadow is placed behind the object it will make us feel like the object is still floating in space but now, this object has a wall behind it.

There are different types and kinds of shadows for every object and different lighting that will get us a different shadow. Round objects have round shadows, square objects have square shadows.

If an object is near a wall, it will have a sharp, high-density shadow. The more the object moves away from the wall, it's shadow will become softer and more transparent. This way, if an object is jumping, the farther the object, the bigger and softer his shadow will get.

No shadow at all could be also a decision. We can find it in the Vermeer's painting, "Woman in Blue Reading a Letter" and "The Milkmaid" and see how he eliminated completely the shadow of the main figure but took care in such a precise and realistic way, of every other objects' shadows.

This makes the women stand out so much that we get the feeling as if she wasn't just another object in the room but something of much higher importance.

- The Milkmaid, Johannes Vermeer, c. 1660 Rijksmuseum

When combining images together, there are a few things I usually make sure of, in order to make the blending as natural as possible, without it feeling "patchy" and forced.

The first thing is the lightning, the second one is the shadow. Every environment has its own shadow and lightning characteristics. If it's an early morning scene when the sun rises, it produces a long sharp shadow, so if I'm going to add an object or even text to that scene, I might want to consider, creating the same kind of shadow for it, to make it blend naturally.

Night scenes for example, usually have a blue tint, so when I need to add an object to a night scene, I add just a bit of blue colour to the object, and maybe a light blue inner shadow for rim light.

If there's snow in the background, it usually produces a light blue, cyan light, look, so it would probably work to add the same kind of tint to our new object we would like to add.

There are many ways to combine images together to make it look natural but these are my own main few things I check first.

The colour and the lighting of the environment I work in, the direction and the density of the shadows considering the weight, and the size of that new element.

- Eight -

Typography Games

Typography is one of the things designers struggle the most with. There are millions of great examples of beautiful typography masterpieces online, but there is no guidance for what is a good typography or what are the steps we should follow with the specific text given in real designers' day to day projects.

Usually working with big companies, especially advertising agencies, I was given a very specific text to work with. There were a lot of times I could negotiate with the copywriter and make some adaptations in the text for the sake of the typography structure and the design itself, by changing a few words that didn't fit my typography design.

In some cases it is impossible and you're pretty much stuck with the text you got, but you can always propose to use a number (1) instead of letters (one) because they just work better, since human beings tend to notice numbers, question marks and exclamation marks much more than other characters.

During the past decade, after watching, creating and being inspired by endless variations of typography tricks and structures, I have noticed that there are certain rules that are used in most cases regarding the topic or the endeavor and we can provide the right emotion for the viewer and make our typography blend much better and natural with the rest of the design.

By choosing the right font we can really enhance or completely destroy the whole feeling of the concept we're trying to create.

There is an endless number of different kinds of fonts for titles, paragraphs, decorated text, serif fonts for printed text and sans-serif, as in "without" in French for digital text, that is going to appear on screens.

Serif is that small extension in every letter on the end of the line. It is believed that our eyes grab the small extensions and it's easier for us to read, in a way that allows our eyes to grab these small extensions and jump from an extension to the next one, from letter to letter, making it easy to read and follow, but this would only work on a printed media.

It is much harder for us to read serif fonts on digital media since our eyes get tired very quickly with this jumping method on a monitor.

When I approach typography I read the text over and over again trying to find the main idea and the most important words I could highlight.

Sometimes I even try to read it out loud, highlighting a certain word, with my voice, trying to see how it sounds like.

Then I would type the text and let the game begin!

If the text is "Grab these awesome discounts before it's too late," usually, I cut out the main important words and Isolate them. Then, I choose only two main fonts for the text.

When I choose two fonts I try to find two as different as possible fonts, The complete opposite of one another, if you like. For the big important words, I choose usually a bold heavy, sometimes a serif font to make it stand out the most.

The second is a less dominant, usually a light sans serif or a handwritten font, but this is just my own favourite combination and the options are endless. We just have to make sure they're as different as possible and they will be easy to read.

The more the fonts are different from one another, the more they will complement each other.

Grab these
AWESOME DISCOUNTS
Before it's too late

I always try to remember where it is going to appear. Is it going to be printed in a newspaper, shown on a billboard, or is it just the Facebook digital ad?

It is extremely crucial to know these things before you make a decision on choosing any font. Obviously, if it's a digital one, we still can use the serif font, but we need to make sure it's not for a paragraph and it is big enough, easy to read and understood well.

I choose 2 completely contrast colours. If I use a bright green for one I would choose a dark red for the other one. If one is cyan, the other would be magenta.

I remember my first "Shapes and Composition" lessons. I remember these rules about different lines and shapes creating different emotions.

We were taught about how a straight line or a box makes us feel stable and steady, while a diagonal line makes us feel movement and energy.

Same rules apply to typography!

Every letter is the whole complex composition which you can use to your benefit. You could enlarge only one letter or one word and make it the base you're creative.

AWESOME
Discounts

If it's a sports-related text you could write it in a diagonal way, making it much more energetic and moving. A curly line makes us feel energetic and wild. it can be used for welcoming titles, dreamy and fantasy scenes etc.

Shapes

When isolating the words, you get lots of different shapes. Every word creates a shape with its font and letters. The title is a shape, the paragraph is a shape and basically, every sentence and every word in our typography creates a shape.

With this in mind, we can create our text as shapes in a composition and just think about creating the right composition, without even thinking about the text and what it means at this stage.

Sometimes, we get so carried away with working on the text, trying to make sense of the sentence and what it means that it damages our design and creative thinking. From time to time, I like to literally make shapes in the size of the letters and try to figure out the composition first.

This trick makes you think out of the box because it makes the text less intimidating and the feeling "I'm pretty stuck with what I got," regarding text, goes away at this point.

If you have blank spaces or holes inside these shapes it is much easier to think about a solution for this spaces like adding some lines, arrows or other decoration to connect the text better with the general concept, whether it's fantasy or prestige, the shape you will add, will guide the whole style and the general feeling of the typography.

- Nine -

Creative State

When I was in my design studies in "Technion", the "History of Art" lecturer said that if one wants to really know and understand art, he must see 1,000 art pieces!

It looks like this applies to almost every field of life. I really believe that if one is exposed to 1000 top designs and award-winning creatives, he would definitely understand much more about design than before. Every ad you see inspires you and gives you new ways of thinking.

Creativity is like a muscle and just like a muscle, you must feed it with protein and exercise. Inspiration is the protein of creativity. The more websites we see, the better we understand about web design. The more creative we see, the more creative we become.

When I watched the movie Tangled, with my girls, I had no idea, this movie will give me so many insights, about the colour meaning in melancholic scenes, like in the scene where the witch stabbed Yujin and he was dying.

The scene was almost without any colour at all and (spoiler alert) the moment he was back alive, the colours were back, within seconds, as if the sun was suddenly shining right through the walls and entered the room, making it bright and colourful again.

If I want to get some ideas about mixing happy colours, making them look amazing but not too clownish, Trolls would be a great inspiration resource for that. The movie Trolls is really a colour bomb, challenging everything we thought about colours and the meaning of glitter.

Double Mind

Our brain has two parts. The right part of the brain is the "Logic" brain which deals with tasks like science and mathematics. The left side is the "Creative" side which is responsible for art and creativity. [15]

There's a saying that one part could actually improve the other and some creative exercises can actually improve our mathematical skills for example. I'm not suggesting I do math exercises to improve creativity, but having a sudoku, crossword puzzle or an arrow word is a great idea for a creative exercise.

One day I wanted to make a painting of my wife as a birthday gift, so I figured I should take a few lessons to improve my painting skills. Last time I remember myself painting was in junior high. When I started to learn painting again, I've noticed that there are a lot of tricks I could implement in design, like the games with shadows and the rules of lightning.

Unconsciously, I've started to consider the lighting and the shadow angle of the buttons and the weight of the typography in my designs. Painting learning has taught me to add highlights to my buttons, refine images and see typography in a whole different perspective.

I've started to add some "overpaint" on visuals and backgrounds to make it work for my designs. If a figure did not point to the direction I wanted it to point, I just manipulated it with "puppet warp" tool or something to make it point where I want it to point.

As a designer, I never thought about these things. Sometimes, we get this "designer" mood that is not so willing to make some adaptation to an image, claiming it's impossible, because it's pressurized, but if we take a few lessons on concept art painting, or even watch some tutorials on YouTube, our skills as designers and creative thinkers, will improve dramatically.

We must never be affraid of trying new things and manipulating the image we work with, to get the best wanted result.

"Design is created with a hammer, not a feather"
— Col Gray, Pixelsink.com

Workspace

One of the most important and underestimated issues is designer's workspace.

In my opinion, creatives' mood and state of mind have a direct reflection on the design. When I am super motivated and full of inspiration, I feel good and nothing bothers me, and this is when I create the best designs that not only they are approved immediately, but also, they get the best results.

On the other hand, when I feel a little down, out of muse or even generally not feeling well it has a straight influence on the design.

During the years, I've been working in all kinds of different workspaces whether a small independent studio with a few designers like myself and big open spaces with a lot of workers working together.

There were times, I've been designing a new building, that was still under construction, there where very designed studios, made completely out of wood and some places had a modern urban feel to them.

I've realised that my designs and creative thinking are very influenced by the surroundings I've been in. When I worked in a small rickety building, hearing my boss screaming all day long, I was artistically blocked and my brain went from being creative to being protective but when I worked in a designed big central advertising agency, I felt like my muse is bursting out of me.

In my opinion, designer's workspace should be "feng shui" designed in a calm and natural way, without any background disturbing sounds like construction works or other workers' talking and screamings in order to create the optimum conditions for the designer, allowing him to create the best work possible.

- Created by Zee Que | Designbolts.com

There is this argument over the years, between Apple, Mac users and PC users about the best computer for designers. Both have a very good point, actually, there are advantages and disadvantages in each one of them.

I've been using PC and only PC for years until one day I've started working with Mac and here's what I think.

It's like the difference between designing on the beach or designing in your home garage with no windows or air. Obviously, it's not the same proportions but I feel that when I work on a Mac I get this clean, fine-tuned vibe and smooth workflow that is translated into muse and inspiration.

There is something about the folder shadows and how things look, feel and move that creates such a unique feel for me when working on a mac.

It doesn't really matter whether we work on a Mac or a PC, big office or a small studio. If we want to be successful with our creatives and designs, we need to take care of our workspace, hardware and software as the first inspirational resource and the most powerful mood changer we have.

Music

Music has always been part of my inspirational resource and I find it much easier and natural to design something with the right background music.

I find it very hard to try designing a spa boutique brand whether it's a website or promotional materials while listening to heavy metal music.

For me, there's "the right" music for every project. Sure, every person has his own taste and every one of us likes a different kind of music, to be honest, I've changed completely my taste in music, during the past 10 years, being a designer.

I've come to an understanding that not every music fits every project. When I was designing motorbike shop website with "30 seconds to mars" it was awesome, but when creating this spa branding, I figured, I should listen to either calm music or no music at all.

So if you follow the spa example I would try to find spa relaxing music and hear it every time I'm working on the project and even if I've just thought about it, trying to come up with an idea, I find it very helpful to put on some relaxing music just to get myself in the mood.

Break

As humans, we all have our less productive days. When I have these days I try to completely take a break from whatever I'm trying to create.

If I get stuck on some concert making and I'm out of ideas, I go outside to cool down and take a break, have some coffee and read a magazine, but there are times this break is a waste of time. I've learned that there are different types of breaks. Some are inspirational and helping us reach our goal and some are a complete destruction, waste of time and making us even more confused.

I've come to an understanding that taking a break at my desk and going to Facebook or reading news is the worst break ever. It doesn't really give me a break as long as I keep sitting in front of the monitor.

The second worst break is the one in which I do get up from the chair, but I don't stop thinking about whatever it is I'm doing. If I keep thinking about it, my mind doesn't really have a break.

When I take a break, I try to completely pause my thoughts about the current assignment. My brain unconsciously still keeps trying to solve it, even when I'm not thinking about it.

You must be familiar with these moments when you don't even think about something and all of a sudden, out of nowhere, your mind automatically comes up with a solution for some problem you could resolve for a long time and suddenly, just like that, you said to yourself:

"Wait a minute! I think I got it!"

It's because our mind keeps thinking and unconsciously trying constantly to solve whatever issue it's given.

We can never know where will we get our next inspiration for our next creative of our next campaign.

It's like a computer working for long hours, suddenly, works much slower, some certain software functions are having problems and stuff generally have some weird bugs. Only after restarting the computer, things go back to normal and magically everything is working again.

It won't help, if we just the log out and log in again. If you're taking a break and your back to the exact same point you were before, it's just like logging out and logging in without the actual restart process, which will not completely clear these temporarily bad files.

If you're back to the same point trying to figure out your way from there even after a break you still have the bad temporary files in your head with the same problems.

The problems can be caused by many "bad temporary files". Maybe because we asked the wrong questions and got the wrong answers or maybe it's because we are not feeling in line with our target audience or maybe it's because this specific field of expertise is not our "cup of tea" or we have never designed or even been exposed to and it feels unnatural trying to force ourselves to design it.

It is very important to understand what it is, that's holding you back in and pauses your muse, make a complete full restart for your brain then go back to the first stage of the asking questions.

If I lose interest in a specific design or endeavor field of expertise, I take my break and then return one step back to my research stage. I search for more inspiration for this field and after I find some, I go back to my design immediately.

I've found out the hard way, that it won't be a good idea for me, taking a break right after the research, because when I'm back from the break I don't feel connected with this field of expertise as much. I must dive right into design right after the "inspirational research".

When I'm stuck usually because I'm out of inspiration or I don't have the right answers to the right questions, so when I'm back from the break, I try to go as back as I can, to the main first questions and try to realise how I've tried to solve them.

Usually, with a fresh mind, I find a solution, during this answering questions process.

"WOW" Elements

During the years, I was trying to find the "perfect" design. I'm starting to realise, there's really no such a thing as perfect, but I've noticed that there are some elements that create the "Wow" reaction out of people when they are being used right.

I was thinking about all scenes I could remember from movies, art, design and real life, trying to find what was in common of these scenes that made me say "Wow!".

Obviously every person has its own memories and nostalgia for things, so it's not that when I add one of these elements, my design immediately gets better, it must be implemented well, considering all rules of design, like colour, typography and composition, but these elements works very well for the majority and usually creates the emotion we desire to create with our target audience.

Motion

Motion is one of the things human tend to notice the most. If the background is static and there's a figure moving, or the figure is focused and static and the background is moving, it's such a contrasted scene that it's almost impossible to ignore.

Waterfalls

Waterfalls are used usually to increase the feeling of the force of nature, its beauty and what it is capable of. I'm not sure what it is about waterfalls, but when it's the main object of your design and it is presented in the right composition and colours, it creates a fascinating effect.

Sunsets

I use it usually for romantic scenes. Our scene doesn't have to be a romantic story between two people, but it can be implemented in such way that will make the observer have a romantic mood and might fall in love with what we try to represent.

Lens Flare

Usually, it comes from sunsets and sunrises. It can also appear on glass or shiny metal and pictures taken by old cameras or video shots.

If I want the observer to notice a specific shiny thing like a coin or a button, I apply "Lens Flare" and place it on the object's edge, which makes it super noticeable and really stands out from the rest. It can also create a vintage effect like it's a feeling of a picture taken by an old camera.

Jungle

Jungle makes you feel wild, free and hidden from civilisation. Jungle could be a really good way to present a feeling of escaping, change your life or hiding.

Fire

Usually used for energetic and dramatic scenes. Creates a sense of power. There is something about fire that makes you feel somehow on the other side and being friends with the bad boys.

Designed by: pinnacleanimates and sirisako

Black and white

There is something very appealing in black-and-white images whether for creating an old vintage feel or a high-class look.

Luxurious products are used in black-and-white a lot, even more than we might notice in advertising, movies and more.

The whole branding identity of a company could use black and white as their guiding colours, usually for luxury brands like Gucci and Versace that use black and white backgrounds in ads and like "Apple", keeping it super clean with black and white minimalism.

Staying Updated

No one is born a creative thinker, neither a designer. These skills come in time with practising and learning constantly, pretty much about everything, because if I'm trying to create some commercial materials for the Saint Patrick's Day sale, I have to be familiar at least a little bit with Saint Patrick's origins which are Irish and I should know just a little bit of the Irish culture, what they do and what they like and what has already been done if I want to create an original campaign. As creative people, we should always be updated with the popular nowadays trends whether it's a very spoken new movie or a new song or a new top model, in my opinion, we should at least acknowledge it and maybe even use it in our next creative.

It is a well-known fact, that the masses get the attracted to something that is very spoken of. That's why advertising companies ask celebrities and well-known figures and influencers to advertise products.

Every movie, book, story and painting can be a source of inspiration for something. Every song we hear influences our mood and can give us an idea for a design. Every trip in nature can give us a new "Wow element" to work with. We as creatives, must watch movies, go on trips in nature, go to parties, visit museums and live our lives for our creative inspiration, trying to stay in this creative state as long as possible. This way, creative thinking will be a part of who we are and will float right out of us in the moment of need.

"Design" is not about creating the best masterpiece that will be remembered for decades. It's about designing the right thing for the right target audience and present it in the right place and the right time.

- Ten -

Summary

C reative thinking might feel like rocket science sometimes, but the truth is that the more we create, the easier it gets. Our minds begin to automatically come up with greater and greater ideas, much faster and faster.

The more we apply design rules and notice them, it becomes natural and easier for us, creating the correct design according to the rules, without even noticing it.

As a student I remember adding the golden ratio shape, trying to make my design fit in that spiral shape, thinking to myself "If I could only find a way to make it fit, it'll be perfect".

The problem is that if we won't take into account other ingredients such as colour theory, the right alignment and so on, the magic formula won't work.

The most brilliant creatives have a great deal of general knowledge which allows them to provide great creatives within seconds, based on the right target audience and how to make them emotional and make them take an action of some kind.

We are living in a beautiful era, in which every piece of information is available at the click of a button. We can find everything about every business and every inspirational resource we can imagine in a second. It used to be very hard to get information about some business or occupational field, especially, trying to get yourself into a community of some kind.

Today all information on all communities went online so now they are very easy to find and it's very easy to join them, understand the language they use, their feelings their problems and their passions.

Great marketing is one that is presented in such way, the target audience gets emotional with it and can't ignore it without feeling spammy. For that, we have to follow this process of finding the answers to the right questions that would be crucial for our success as creatives, hitting the right target, whether we're working on a private label of a small company or a huge corporation brand, the same rules apply to every business.

If we know the right questions to be asked, we will come up with great creatives that will provide lots of emotions for the target audience that will be willing to take action.

If we want to draw people's attention we can use visual tricks that were used by the greatest long ago, but we must not be afraid to try new things.

In the branding process, when designing a logo there's a stage, I like to call "10 logo speed sketch". It's the stage right after the "Inspirational research" when the designer starts designing the logo by sketching ideas on a paper.

There's a saying that suggests to limit yourself with time and sketch 10 different logos in 5 minutes or less for a logo. This way we force ourselves to think fast, out of the box and we don't fall in love with our first sketch.

Perfection is our worst enemy as creatives. There's no "perfect design" that will work for everyone. Just like some interpret red as danger and others might see it, as the colour of love.

In my opinion, we're only at the beginning of the understanding of the human mind and its passions. We can never know what will be the best next thing or the next token trend. It could be a new composition guideline or some interesting new colour combination (like the new iOS 7 colour palette back in 2013).

We have to constantly try to push ourselves into trying new things, by ourselves. The market will decide if it works for him. When the market likes something, we must be familiar with it and try it out, in our designs, if we want to present a vibe of an updated business that follows trends. If our audience likes something we must embrace it and never fight it, even if we didn't like it much.

One of my teachers stated that there's the personal taste of the target audience, which we must follow, and there's the personal taste of our clients that, it would be nice to follow (especially if it's inlined with the target audience's taste). And then, there's our personal taste of the designer, that we must never follow.

The main thing here is to listen to our target audience as much as possible, understand their needs and trends, understand the place they're going to meet us (Facebook, Instagram etc.) and get them to have the right emotions, whether by the right colour, a creative story or a great composition, leading their eyes and cursor to the right place of taking action.

When we present something in the right way, it becomes a problem solver and a solution for our target audience, providing a solution to their exact problem, instead of just another spammy ad.

- Eleven -

About the Author

Mark Zusmanovich was born in 1984 in Azerbaijan, part of the Soviet Union, in that time, and immigrated with his family to Israel at the age of 5 in 1989.

Mark finished the matriculation examination with graphic design, as the main increased subject, before going on to earn the academic degree of "Practical Engineer" from the Technion – Israel Institute of Technology, for Interactive Communication Engineering studies that included subjects such as design, art, animation, video editing, sound and user experience.

He is a Digital Marketing Designer for the past 10 years, as a self-employed designer and in advertising worldwide agencies with clients such as Nike, Toyota, Intel, Champion Motors and more.

He has been solving design challenges and creating marketing and advertising concepts, along with top creative managers, art directors and copywriters.

Mark specialises in creating marketing strategies, mainly for small and medium businesses, providing different kinds of services, such as branding, marketing strategy planning, marketing concepts and motion graphics.

Member of the Nonfiction Authors Association.

Feel free to contact me and let me know what you think about this book: mark@pentocreative.com

- Twelve -

References

1. Hyerle (2000), Visual Teaching Alliance, Why Visual Teaching? <http://visualteachingalliance.com>

2. Jeff Bullas (no date), 6 Powerful Reasons Why you Should include Images in your Marketing <https://www.jeffbullas.com/6-powerful-reasons-why-you-should-include-images-in-your-marketing-infographic>

3. Drucker, Peter (1954), The practice of management. New York: Harper and Row Publishers.

4. Curiosity Staff (September 16th, 2016), A 1864 Telegram Was The World's First Spam Message <https://curiosity.com/topics/a-1864-telegram-was-the-worlds-first-spam-message-curiosity>

5. Content Marketing Institute (September 9th, 2015), Documentary - The Story of Content: Rise of the New Marketing <https://www.youtube.com/watch?v=dBnpr3pkFlk>

6. Gary vaynerchuk (January 2018), How to tell a story on social media <https://www.garyvaynerchuk.com/how-to-tell-a-story-on-social-media>

7. Wikipedia, the free encyclopedia (no date) <https://en.wikipedia.org/wiki/Designer>

8. Wikipedia, the free encyclopedia (no date) <https://en.wikipedia.org/wiki/Art#cite_note-OD-1>

9. By 迪蹼弎 (March 4th 2015) [CC BY-SA 4.0 (https://creativecommons.org/licenses/by-sa/4.0)], from Wikimedia Commons <https://upload.

wikimedia.org/wikipedia/commons/d/db/34%2A21-FibonacciBlocks.png>

10. Beck, Matthias; Geoghegan, Ross (2010), The Art of Proof: Basic Training for Deeper Mathematics, New York: Springer.

Bóna, Miklós (2011), A Walk Through Combinatorics (3rd ed.), New Jersey: World Scientific.

11. Blender Guru, Understanding Composition (October 15th, 2014) <https://www.youtube.com/watch?v=O8i7OKbWmRM>

12. By MinoZig (September 18th 2015) [CC BY-SA 4.0 (https://creativecommons.org/licenses/by-sa/4.0)], from Wikimedia Commons

<https://commons.wikimedia.org/wiki/File:Deathstalker_(Leiurus_quinquestriatus)_6.jpg>

13. By Kwamikagami (September 9th 2015) [CC BY-SA 4.0 (https://creativecommons.org/licenses/by-sa/4.0)], from Wikimedia Commons <https://commons.wikimedia.org/wiki/File:Color_star-en_(tertiary_names).svg>

14. Joseph J. Krakora (2001), Vermeer: Master of Light <https://www.youtube.com/watch?v=DEior-oinxU>

15. The Brain Made Simple, (no date) <http://brainmadesimple.com/left-and-right-hemispheres.html>